Healthy Me

Keeping Clean

Ryan Wheatcroft   Katie Woolley

Leabharlanna Poiblí Chathair Baile Átha Cliath
Dublin City Public Libraries

WAYLAND

First published in Great Britain in 2017 by Wayland

Copyright © Hodder and Stoughton, 2017

Editor: Victoria Brooker
Designer: Anthony Hannant, Little Red Ant

ISBN: 978 1 5263 0555 8 (hbk)
ISBN: 978 1 5263 0556 5 (pbk)

10 9 8 7 6 5 4 3 2 1

Wayland, an imprint of
Hachette Children's Group
Part of Hodder and Stoughton
Carmelite House
50 Victoria Embankment
London EC4Y 0DZ

An Hachette UK Company
www.hachette.co.uk
www.hachettechildrens.co.uk

Printed and bound in China

FSC
www.fsc.org
MIX
Paper from
responsible sources
FSC® C104740

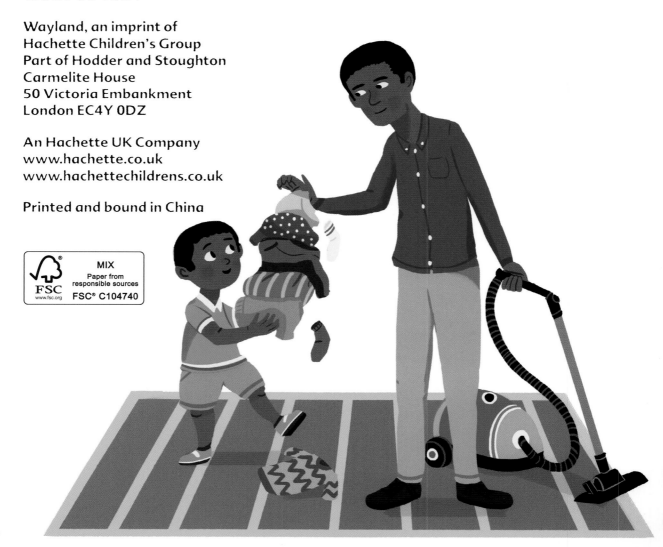

Contents

Your Amazing Body

Your body is a pretty amazing thing — every day it works hard to digest food, pump oxygen to your muscles and keep you fit and active. But your body sometimes needs a little help.

Keeping clean is one way of helping your body stay healthy. You look better, smell better and feel good about yourself when you look after your body. The more you keep clean, the healthier you will be.

Germs Everywhere

Keeping clean is important because it helps protect you from germs. You can't see germs but they are everywhere. Germs live on door handles, on your clothes and even on your skin.

Your skin is the biggest organ in your body and it has an important job to do. It keeps you warm in the winter and cool in the summer. It also keeps your insides in and germs out. You need to look after it!

Feeling Sick

Sometimes, even when you do keep clean, germs get inside your body. These germs can cause infections. You may catch a cold, get a cough, have a fever or even feel sick for a little while.

Most germs are spread through the air by sneezes and coughs but they are also in body fluids, such as sweat and saliva. Breathing germs in or touching something or someone with those germs can pass them on. The best way to avoid getting sick is to keep clean.

Clean Hands

The best way to keep germs at bay is to wash your hands. It's important to wash them after you cough and sneeze. Always wash your hands after you have been to the toilet, and before you are about to eat or cook some food.

1. SOAP

2. WASH

3. RINSE

4. DRY

When you wash your hands, use warm water and soap and rub your hands together for about 15 seconds. That's as long as it takes to sing 'Happy Birthday' twice.

Clean Hair

It's not just your skin that needs to be kept clean. Your hair gets dirty, too. Hair grows out of hair follicles. These follicles are attached to glands that make an oil to keep your hair shiny.

Sweat glands on your head release sweat, and dead skin cells come off on to your scalp, too. All this oil, sweat and dead skin makes your hair dirty. Washing your hair regularly keeps it clean and healthy.

Clean Teeth

Strong, healthy teeth are a vital part of your body. They help you tear, cut and chew your food. They also look great when you smile. "Cheese!"

Bacteria, called plaque, stick to your teeth and gums.
They can cause toothache, painful gums and even
bad breath. Brushing your teeth for two minutes,
twice a day, will help to keep bacteria away.

Clean Feet

Your feet are very busy all day — they help you stand, walk, run and play. They get hot and sweaty, and sometimes smelly! Bacteria love the sweat, oil and dead skin cells on your feet.

Wash your feet regularly and dry them properly afterwards. Put on clean socks each morning and wear shoes that aren't too tight.

Noses and Nails

Dirt and germs love to hide. Luckily, it's the job of sticky stuff called mucus, or snot, to trap germs in your nose and stop them getting any further. Picking your nose isn't a good idea because snot is full of these germs. Give your nose a blow instead!

Dirt and germs also get under your nails. In fact, there are more bacteria under your fingernails than under a toilet seat! To keep your hands and feet clean, wash them often and cut your nails once a week.

Easy Ears

Without your ears, you wouldn't be able to hear the trees rustling in the wind or listen to your favourite music. You need to keep your ears clean and healthy. Gently wash the outside with soap and water when you have a bath or a shower.

Inside your ear is a sticky substance called earwax. You might think earwax is dirty but it really isn't! It's got an important job to do. Earwax protects your ear canal, so leave it in your ears.

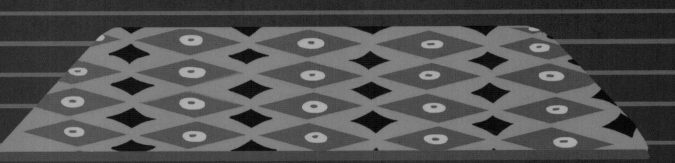

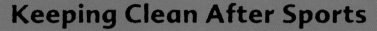

Keeping Clean After Sports

Exercise is an important part of being healthy. When you exercise your body sweats, and dirt and toxins are released. The best way to get rid of these toxins is to have a wash.

It's great fun to play outside but the outdoors can be messy! Just think of how muddy you are after a game of football or a walk in the woods! Once you've finished having fun outside, it's time to wash and get clean.

Clean Clothes

You wear clothes every day and they soon get grubby, especially your underclothes. Put on clean socks and underwear each morning. Clothes collect dead skin cells, sweat and other dirt all day long.

Wearing clean clothes and underwear will help to keep your body clean. Also wear shoes that aren't too tight, as this could make your feet sweat more than usual.

Keep your shoes clean by brushing or washing them regularly, so they don't begin to smell!

Why Do I Need to Clean My Room?

It isn't just your body and your clothes that can get dirty. Your house needs to be clean, too. Dust mites are tiny bugs that live in household dust. You can't see them but they are there!

Dust mites get into pillows, blankets, mattresses and soft toys. Keeping your bedroom clean and tidy keeps these pesky mites at bay. You spend a lot of time in your bedroom so the cleaner it is, the cleaner your body will be!

Top Tips!

Always wash
your hands after
you've been
to the toilet.

Don't pick earwax
from your ears. If you
think your ears are
blocked with wax, visit
your doctor who will be
able to help.

Don't leave dirty clothes on your bedroom floor. Pick them up and put in the wash basket! The cleaner your room is the cleaner you will be.

Fluoride in your toothpaste keeps your teeth clean. It mixes with the hard coating on your teeth, called enamel, and helps to protect them against plaque. Less plaque means strong, healthy teeth, so brush, brush, brush!

Parents' and Teachers' Notes

This book is designed for children to begin to learn about the importance of being healthy, and the ways in which we can look after our bodies to keep clean and well. Read the book with children either individually or in groups. Don't forget to talk about the pictures as you go.

A clean body is very important for keeping illnesses at bay and for feeling good about yourself. Creating good hygiene habits from an early age is vital. Here are some discussion topics to encourage further thinking about keeping clean:

 Why is it important to have clean bodies?

 What is the first thing you do in the morning to get clean and ready for school?

 When you have a bath, what parts of your body need to be cleaned?

 Why do we have teeth? What do they help us do each day? (Talking, chewing, smiling etc.)

Activities you can do:

 Act out how you wash your face and hands, clean your hair and brush your teeth.

 Why not write a poem about keeping clean, like this one:

Wash, wash, wash. I'm nice and clean.
I'll brush my teeth so they gleam.
Soap and lather everywhere.
Lots of bubbles in my hair!

Further reading

All By Myself: Bubbles, Tub, Have a Scrub by Debbie Foy (Wayland, 2015)
Let's Read and Talk About Keeping Clean by Honor Head (Franklin Watts, 2015)
Looking After Me: Keeping Clean by Liz Gogerly (Wayland, 2014)
Wonderwise: Wash, Scrub, Brush! by Brita Granstrom and Mick Manning (Franklin Watts, 2014)

Glossary

bacteria tiny living things that are all around you. Most bacteria
can only be seen with a microscope

digest to break down food

ear canal the tube that runs from the outside of your ear to the middle ear.
The ear canal lets in sound so you can hear.

earwax a yellow-brown substance that is made by glands in the ear canal

follicle a tube-like cavity, sac or gland

germ a tiny living thing that can cause harm to plants, animals and humans

gland tissues or organs of the body that produce a substance that helps
the body to function properly

muscle a part of the body that helps the body move

organ the part of a person, plant or animal that has a specific function

oxygen a gas in the air

plaque a substance that builds up on your teeth and can cause decay

scalp the skin on your head, usually covered with hair

toxin a poisonous waste material produced by the body

Index